D1736003

The Gospel of

LUKE

Studies in This Series
Available from your Christian book store:

How to Start a Neighborhood Bible Study
A Guide to Discussion Study

Mark

Luke

The Acts of the Apostles

Romans

1 Corinthians
Challenge to Maturity

2 Corinthians and Galatians
A Call for Help and Freedom

A Study of Ephesians and Philemon

Philippians and Colossians
Letters from Prison

The Letter to the Hebrews

1 and 2 Peter
Letters to People in Trouble

The First Epistle of John and the Epistle of James

They Met Jesus
Eight Studies of New Testament Characters

Four Men of God
Abraham, Joseph, Moses, David

Psalms and Proverbs

Choose Life
Basic Doctrines of the Christian Faith
Available from Neighborhood Bible Studies,
Dobbs Ferry, New York 10522

Conversations with Jesus Christ
from the Gospel of John

Patterns for Living with God
Twelve Old Testament Character Studies

The Gospel of
LUKE

13 Discussions for Group Bible Study

by Marilyn Kunz and Catherine Schell

TYNDALE HOUSE PUBLISHERS
Wheaton, Illinois

Front cover photo of the city of Nazareth,
courtesy of Israel Government Tourist Office

Library of Congress Catalog Card Number 72-97661
ISBN 8423-3880-2

Copyright © 1973 by Neighborhood Bible Studies, Inc.
All rights reserved

Sixth printing, September 1978
Printed in the United States of America

Contents

How to Use This Discussion Guide

1/ *For groups using a rotating leadership* — Each person *must* read this page *before* leading a study from this guide.

2/ *The purpose of this study guide* — To help the discussion leader guide others to discover for themselves the facts, the meaning and the application to personal life of the Gospel of Luke, paragraph by paragraph.

3/ *Discussion questions* — This guide provides the discussion leader with questions for the three basic areas of investigation — facts, meaning, and application. There are more questions provided than the leader will need, so he must *select* the questions which will help his group to cover the main point of each paragraph. Focus attention on the chapter of the Bible, *not* on the study guide. An alert group will answer many of the suggested questions before they are asked. *Avoid* going woodenly through each and every question.

If everyone in the group has his own copy of the guide and has used it in study preparation for the discussion, it will be possible to discuss the contents and meaning of the passage in greater depth within the time available to the group.

The leader should never answer his own questions. He must be alert to avoid becoming a lecturer instead of a discussion leader. However, after others have made their contributions in answer to a question, the leader may add his own findings and/or restate some of the important points made by others. Sometimes a group needs *more time* than the leader realizes in order to find the answer to the questions. Sometimes the group needs a secondary or *supplementary question* such as the study guide amply provides in order to get to the heart of the paragraph.

4/ Most of the discussions on Luke's Gospel will include two chapters per study. This means that each minor point of a chapter *cannot* be dealt with in detail. Rather, the group should move through the study by the sections indicated, some of which may include several paragraphs. If individual members will read the chapters in Luke carefully and work through the study guide questions before coming to the group discussion, then the group can move quickly enough over larger sections of the material to accomplish the indicated chapters each time.

5/ *The summary questions* — These endeavor to give *perspective* to the study of the chapter. Do not neglect or rush over the summary questions.

6/ *Reading the chapter aloud* — The chapters from the Bible should be read aloud by paragraphs at the start of the group study. Though people will have studied the chapter during the week they will need to refresh their memory in order to enter fully into the discussion. Be sure to have the reading done by paragraphs or thought units, *never* verse by verse. It is not necessary for everyone to read aloud, or for each to read an equal amount.

The reading may be done in one of two ways: read a whole chapter aloud before discussing the questions paragraph by paragraph, or read a paragraph or section aloud and discuss that portion before reading the next portion. This latter method is helpful in those chapters where there is little connection between paragraphs or larger sections.

7/ *Use of contemporary translations of the Bible* — It is strongly recommended that everyone have at least one recent translation of the Bible in addition to the King James Version or Douay Version. The questions in this study guide assume the availability of a contemporary translation.

8/ There is a *map* on page 64 of this study guide. Locate the places mentioned as you study each chapter.

Sharing Leadership Why and How

Each study guide in the Neighborhood Bible Study series is

prepared with the intention that the ordinary adult group will be able by using this guide to rotate the leadership of the discussion. Those who are outgoing in personality are more likely to volunteer to lead first, but within a few weeks it should be possible for almost everyone to have the privilege of directing a discussion session. Everyone, including people new to the Bible who may not yet have committed themselves to Christ, should be encouraged to take a turn in leading by asking questions from the study guide.

Reasons for this approach are:

1. The discussion leader will prepare in greater depth than the average participant.

2. The experience of leading a study stimulates a person to be a better participant in the discussions led by others.

3. Members of the group which changes discussion leadership weekly tend to feel that the group belongs to everyone in it. It is not "Mr. or Mrs. Smith's Bible Study."

4. The Christian who by reason of spiritual maturity and wider knowledge of the Bible is equipped to be a spiritual leader in the group is set free to *listen* to everyone in the group in a way that is not possible when leading the discussion. He (she) takes his regular turn in leading as it comes around, but if he leads the first study in a series he must guard against the temptation to bring a great deal of outside knowledge and source material which would make others feel they could not possibly attempt to follow his example of leadership.

Discussion Bible Study — Advantages and Methods

What are the advantages of discussion study?

1/ People studying the Bible for the first time are often more willing to attend a discussion study than to submit to the authority of a teacher.

2/ A discussion Bible study gives opportunity for each participant to voice his questions and problems as he reacts to the passage under consideration.

3/ The degree of participation is much higher in a discussion than in a lecture form of study. Consequently there tends to be greater learning on the part of each discussion member.

What is the function of this study guide?

1/ The study guide helps a group to make new discoveries together. It directs the group into the main points of the chapter, and prevents aimless wandering and consequent wasting of time.

2/ The study guide makes it possible for each member of the group to take his turn in leading the discussion. The leader does not have to be able to lecture to the group or to explain the meaning of everything in the chapter. Rather he guides the group through the Bible passage by asking the questions from the study guide. Rotation of leadership from week to week results in greater participation and learning for each person in the group.

A group in which the discussion leadership is equally shared can continue even after the person who first initiated the group moves to another area.

What rules make for an effective discussion?

1/ Everyone in the group should *read the Bible passage* and, if possible, use the study guide in thoughtful *study* of the passage *before* coming to the group meeting.

2/ *Stick to the Bible passage under discussion.* Discover all that you can from this section of Luke's Gospel without moving around to other books of the Bible in cross-references. This means that the person new to the Bible will not be needlessly confused, and you will avoid the danger of taking portions out of context.

3/ As your group proceeds through the Gospel of Luke, you will *build a common frame of reference.* Within a few weeks it will be possible for people to refer back to several chapters of Luke and to trace lines of thought through large sections of his Gospel.

4/ *Avoid tangents.* Many different ideas will be brought to mind as you study each chapter of Luke. If an idea is not dealt with in any detail in a particular section, do not let it occupy long discussion that week. Appoint a recorder in your group to make note of this and other such questions that arise from week to week. As your group studies on in the book of Luke, you will find some of these questions are answered in later chapters.

5/ Since the three-fold purpose of an inductive Bible study is to discover what the Bible portion says, what it means, and what it means to you, your group should remember that *the Gospel of Luke is the authority for your study*. The aim of your group should be to discover what Luke is saying, to discover Luke's message.

If you don't like something that Luke says, be honest enough to admit that you don't like it. Do not rewrite the Bible to make it agree with your ideas. You may say that you do not agree with Luke, or that you wish he had not said this, but don't try to make him say what he does not say. It is Luke's account that you are investigating. Let him state his own case.

6/ *Apply to your own life what you discover in the study of Luke's Gospel.* Much of the vitality of any group Bible discussion depends upon honest sharing on the part of different members of the group. Discoveries made in Bible study should become guides for right action in present day life situations.

Jesus is presented ever more clearly as Luke moves through his account, so that you have the opportunity to see the evidence Luke considered certain proof that Jesus is the Christ of God. You have the opportunity to face the implications for your life of Jesus' claims.

7/ *Let honesty with love be the attitude of your group toward one another.* Those who do not believe that Jesus is the Christ should be able to voice their doubts and questions without feeling rejected or feeling that they should cover up their true feelings. Those who do believe and are committed to Jesus as Lord and Savior should be free to share how this belief affects their lives (as appropriate to the section of Luke under discussion). Rather than trying to convince one another of your beliefs or disbeliefs, you should let yourself be searched and judged by the Gospel of Luke. You should examine Luke's account for yourself.

Introduction to the Gospel of Luke

The Gospel of Luke is part one of a two-volume work, *Luke — Acts,* in which the writer covers the period of Jesus' life, death and resurrection, and the first thirty years of the Christian Church. His historical account ties the New Testament together, the Gospel of Luke dealing with the same events as the other Gospels and the Acts of the Apostles giving the historical setting for Paul's letters.

Luke was a Gentile (so far as we know, the only Gentile among the New Testament writers), a medical doctor by profession (Colossians 4:14), and a native of Antioch in Syria, according to a second-century tradition. He accurately sets his account in the context of the Roman world, dating the events of *Luke — Acts* by numerous references to Roman emperors and governors. A companion of the Apostle Paul, Luke had ample opportunity to do research for his Gospel account during Paul's two-year imprisonment in Caesarea (Acts 24:27). Jerusalem and Galilee lay within two days' travel so that Luke would have had access to eyewitnesses of the Gospel events.

Luke's profession of medicine may explain his special interest in the events surrounding the birth of John the Baptist and the virgin birth of Jesus as well as his careful description of the physical resurrection of Jesus. Throughout his Gospel Luke mentions needy people — the poor, the outcasts, the lost, and he represents Jesus as the deliverer and redeemer, the One who brings and who is the Good News.

Discussion 1 / Luke 1, 2

The Birth of Jesus

Luke's opening paragraph is in the style and language of the great Greek historians. He devotes his first two chapters to establishing the uniqueness of Jesus by his description of divine intervention in the births of John and Jesus.

Luke 1:1-4

1. What is the source of Luke's information for his Gospel? What is his method and motive in writing this account?

Luke 1:5-25

2. How does Luke provide clues for dating the events in his document from both civil and religious sources?
3. From verses 5-13 describe Zechariah and Elizabeth. Note at least seven things about them.
4. What specifically does the angel foretell about the son Elizabeth will bear Zechariah? On what facts does Zechariah base his response to the angel's message?
5. What does Zechariah's question (verse 18) suggest about his confidence in the angel's reliability? How is his question answered (verses 19-25)?
6. Why do we find the promises of God difficult to believe? Why and how do we limit God to our own resources?

Luke 1:26-38

7. Describe briefly the encounter between Mary and the angel Gabriel. Compare Mary's reaction to Gabriel with that of Zechariah. What similarities and what differences do you observe in their reactions? Consider the difference in what is

promised to Mary and to Zechariah, and what is required from each.

8. Make a list in two parallel columns of what is foretold about John (verses 14-17) and Jesus (verses 32-35). Compare these predictions.

Luke 1:39-56

9. What happens when Mary visits her relative Elizabeth? Why do you think that Luke includes this description of that visit? What is the significance of Elizabeth's statement (verse 43)?

Luke 1:57-80

10. Describe the events surrounding the birth of John. What does his father foretell about John's ministry? From Gabriel's message (verses 14-17) and what Zechariah says (verses 68-79), make a list of the expectations you might have as to what John would be and do.

Luke 2:1-21

11. What prevents Jesus' being born at home in Nazareth? (See also Micah 5:2.)

12. What events of Jesus' birth apparently are ordinary? What are extraordinary? What message do the shepherds receive? What command to them is implied?

Luke 2:22-52

13. Describe briefly the three trips to Jerusalem mentioned in this section. What is the purpose and outcome of each journey?

14. What have Jesus' parents learned about him from the shepherds, from Simeon, and from his own words and actions?

15. How does verse 40 summarize the childhood of Jesus? How do verses 51, 52 summarize his youth? What elements are emphasized in both sections?

SUMMARY

1. To what people and events in secular history does Luke

relate the events of Jesus' birth? Why is it important that he sets his account in historical context, both for the people to whom he wrote originally, and those who would read his account many centuries later?

2. How does Luke indicate that Jesus was conceived without any action of a human father (a virgin birth)? See also Matthew 1:18-21.

3. Summarize from these chapters what was foretold about the ministry of John and the ministry of Jesus. State in a sentence what each was going to do.

4. In what ways did God prove himself trustworthy to those involved in the events associated with the birth of John and Jesus?

CHOICES

The choices we have in life include how we will respond to the activity and will of God. Zechariah and Elizabeth chose to act in faith when God said he was going to answer their prayers for a son. Mary chose to accept the awesome plan God had for her life. Was she tempted to say as some of us do, "Not I, Lord!"? The shepherds chose to obey the angelic message to go and see for themselves. Simeon and Anna decided that they would believe and proclaim the revelation that the infant Jesus was the Lord's Christ.

How do you choose to respond to the fact of Jesus' coming?

Discussion 2 / Luke 3, 4

John's Ministry; Jesus' Temptation and Early Preaching

Years of silence intervene in Luke's account between chapters 2 and 3. About thirty years (3:23) have passed since the events of the birth of John and his cousin Jesus as John begins the ministry his father Zechariah prophesied for him.

Luke 3:1-14

1. Into what historical setting does Luke put John's ministry? What has the prophet Isaiah foretold about John and his ministry (verses 4-6)?
2. What warning does John give? How does this preaching fulfill the predicted purpose of his ministry?
3. What does John mean when he tells his Jewish audience, "Don't say, 'We have Abraham as our father' "? What does God want from men? What kinds of people respond to John's warnings, and what instructions does he give them?

Luke 3:15-38

4. What question of identity does the ministry of John provoke and how does he answer it? Compare verse 15 with Luke 2:11, 26.
5. How and why is John's ministry ended? What, do you think, is the significance of the events at Jesus' baptism? What does verse 22b add to our knowledge of Jesus from 2:40, 52?
6. Why, do you think, does Luke give Jesus' genealogy at this point rather than with the description of his birth? Instead of following Jesus' lineage back only to Abraham, founder of the Jewish people, how far does Luke trace it? What emphasis does he accomplish by this?

Luke 4:1-4

7. From verses 1, 2, how do you know that the temptation of Jesus is within the will of God? What do you understand to be the difference between temptation and sin?

8. Someone has pointed out that most people never experience the pressure of long temptation because they succumb so soon. What does the fact that Jesus does not eat during this period add to our understanding of the severity of this whole testing experience?

9. On what levels does the devil attack Jesus in verse 3? Why is the challenge more potent than saying, "If you are hungry"? Would the challenge to change a stone to bread be a temptation to you? Why not? What does this imply about Jesus' power?

10. What is the resource Jesus uses to overcome this temptation? What does this indicate about the worthwhileness of memorizing Scripture? What does Jesus mean by his answer (verse 4)?

Luke 4:5-8

11. What does the devil promise Jesus and what does he demand from him in return? What does this mean? Why would this temptation be especially powerful as Jesus approaches his public ministry? How does Jesus meet this particular test?

12. Why is it important that Jesus know clearly the direction his life should take? If you worship and serve the Lord God only, what other "gods" and "lords" will you have to give up?

Luke 4:9-13

13. What new form does the temptation take in verse 10? What warning should this be to us about accepting anything which is said simply because Scripture is quoted with it?

14. What is the meaning of this temptation? How is a concern for our own importance often a source of temptation? How do you know that Jesus experienced temptation again?

15. How does it help you to realize that Jesus has ex-

perienced temptation? Fit each of the following areas of possible temptation into one of the three temptations which Jesus overcame: a concern about personal identity; a deep physical need; a desire to succeed in a job; compromise for a "good" purpose; who am I?; can God answer my need?; is God there?; do your own thing.

Luke 4:14-30

16. Describe Jesus' ministry in Nazareth. What pleases the people of his home town? What angers them? Why? How do they express their anger?

Luke 4:31-44

17. Describe Jesus' ministry in Capernaum. What authority and what power does he have? What pattern develops in Jesus' confrontation with demons? Why?

18. In spite of his activity of healing and of casting out demons, what does Jesus say is his major purpose? How could his power to heal become a source of temptation to Jesus?

SUMMARY

1. If you had been a reporter on the scene, how would you have described the ministry of John and the early ministry of Jesus? What particular incidents or quotations would you have put in your article? Why?

2. What do you learn about how to handle temptation in your own life from Luke's description of the temptation of Jesus? When should we expect temptation? How can we recognize it? What can we do about it?

CHOICES

The ministry of John gave many people the opportunity to choose whether they would repent, confess their sins and prepare to welcome the Lord. Jesus had choices to make as to how he would respond to the devil's temptations. The choices Jesus made then make a difference in my life today.

Discussion 3 / Luke 5, 6

The Call and Training of the Twelve

Jesus' preaching and healing ministry includes here the call and training of particular men to be his disciples (followers) and then his apostles (messengers).

Luke 5:1-11

1. What does Luke emphasize in this paragraph instead of describing what Jesus teaches? Why?
2. Why is Peter so moved by their big catch? What does he recognize about Jesus, about himself?
3. What difference does it make that Jesus first helps Peter and the others to succeed in their job, rather than calling them to give up fishing while things are not going well? Although Jesus is concerned about Peter's job, to what higher responsibility does he call him?
4. Why don't Peter and the others try to get Jesus to go into the fishing business with them rather than going into Jesus' "business" with him? Do we sometimes do the former? How?

Luke 5:12-26

5. Compare the two incidents in this section as to location, witnesses of the event, problems dealt with, Jesus' actions, and the results. What does Jesus prove about himself in these incidents?
6. Into what category do the Jewish religious leaders (Pharisees and teachers of the law) put Jesus' claim to forgive sins? How does Jesus prove that he does have the authority to forgive sins? What is the reaction of those who watch the incident?

Luke 5:27-32

7. What are Levi's first actions as a disciple of Jesus? Why don't the religious leaders approve of Jesus' association with these people?

8. Where may we find the people today who are most receptive to Jesus? How can we help them to meet him?

Luke 5:33-39

9. What new complaint is made and why? What old conformity are Jesus' disciples not following? Why? Why can't the new be forced into the old traditional forms? From Jesus' illustrations, what happens because of the vitality of the new if you try to make it fit into old ways? What tends to be the attitude (verse 39) of those accustomed to the old ways of religious expression?

Luke 6:1-11

10. How do these two incidents on the sabbath illustrate further Jesus' teaching in 5:36-38?

11. What specific claim about himself does Jesus make in this first incident?

12. In the second incident what new element comes into the religious leaders' approach to Jesus? Why are they so angry?

Luke 6:12-19

13. What do you think Jesus prays about at such length (verse 12)? Note that Jesus chooses from a larger group of followers (disciples) a select group of twelve to be his apostles (messengers).

14. Describe the crowd which gathers to hear Jesus. (Where do they come from? What do they want?) What does Jesus do for them?

Luke 6:20-26

15. Make parallel lists of the blessings and the woes Jesus proclaims to those who have come to hear him. Who is

blessed and why? To whom is woe pronounced and why? To whom in the past is each group compared?

Luke 6:27-38

16. What standard of conduct does Jesus set before his disciples in the eight situations described in verses 27-30? What principle (verse 31) is to be the guide for all of our conduct toward other people?

17. What three things do sinners do? What are we to do and why? Note — "You will *be sons of* the Most High" is a Jewish way of saying that such people will *be like* the Most High God.

18. How is mercy further illustrated in verses 37, 38? What is the promised result?

Luke 6:39-49

19. What is the major point of each of the three parables in verses 39-42, 43-45 and 46-49?

20. How is hypocrisy defined in these parables? What tests of discipleship are suggested? Why is *hearing* Jesus' teaching not enough?

SUMMARY

1. In these two chapters Luke describes the call and training of the apostles. If you had been one of them, what event or teaching would particularly stick in your mind? Why?

2. What does following Jesus mean in your life today?

CHOICES

Peter, Levi and the other disciples had to choose how to respond to the call of Jesus. They chose to leave *all* to follow him. Today those who follow Jesus have daily choices as to whether or not they will obey and serve him.

Discussion 4 / Luke 7, 8

Desperate Situations

In this section Jesus reveals new facets of his power over severe illness, death, evil spirits, and the forces of nature. He answers John's poignant questions about his identity, and travels and preaches the kingdom of God.

Luke 7:1-17

1. List the different factors which enter into the healing of the centurion's slave. List the factors which lead to the widow's son being returned to life. What would you say is the key factor in the case of the slave? in the case of the widow's son?

2. What are the reactions to the incident at Nain? What do the two incidents in this section add to your understanding of the scope of Jesus' power?

Luke 7:18-35

3. How and why is John reintroduced into Luke's narrative? As John, still imprisoned, hears of Jesus' ministry, what question begins to trouble him? What is the meaning of his questions to Jesus?

4. What answer does Jesus send to John? Compare with Isaiah 29:18, 19; 35:5, 6. In one word, how does Jesus answer John's question of Jesus' identity?

5. What does Jesus teach about John and about people's response to John? How is John more than a prophet?

6. Why do you think those who responded positively to John's ministry would also respond well to Jesus' ministry? How does this influence their reaction (verses 29, 30) to Jesus' comments about John?

7. In what ways is the people's response to John and Jesus compared to that of petulant children?

Luke 7:36-50

8. How are Simon the Pharisee and this woman contrasted in terms of life style, spiritual experience and response to Jesus? What objections do Simon and his friends have in verses 39 and 49? What is the point of the story Jesus tells Simon?

9. The woman is aware of her spiritual need and Simon is not, but according to Jesus' story, both are debtors. What is the answer for them and for us in our spiritual need?

Luke 8:1-15

10. Luke mentions many women in chapters 7, 8, not only those whom Jesus helps, but also those who serve him. What picture do you get of Jesus' itinerant ministry from verses 1-3?

11. What four types of people are described in this parable of the sower and the soils? Although all *hear* the word of God, why are the results different? What things prevent you or people you know from being receptive to God's word?

Luke 8:16-18

12. How does Jesus continue to emphasize the importance of how one hears? What happens to the one who pays attention to Jesus' teachings? to the one who does not pay attention?

Luke 8:19-25

13. What do Jesus' family and/or disciples learn from these incidents? What clues are given as to who Jesus is? Upon what is a relationship with him based? What new range of power does Jesus demonstrate?

Luke 8:26-39

14. Try to imagine yourself as one of the people in this area opposite Galilee. How do you feel about the man with demons? Why are you afraid when he is delivered from them? Why would you want Jesus to leave?

15. What pattern do you observe today in people who pre-

fer physical human solutions to community problems? Why do many fear spiritual solutions? What does it cost to have this man in his right mind? What commission does Jesus give him? How does he fulfill it?

Luke 8:40-56

16. What part does faith have in the experience of Jairus and of the woman with the flow of blood? What are the facts each has to face? What does each have faith in?

17. Comment on the statement, "It is the object of your faith, not the amount of your faith, which makes the difference."

SUMMARY

1. What did Jesus do for the "important" people who came to him: the centurion; Simon the Pharisee; Jairus, ruler of the synagogue? Comparing the centurion and Simon, which knew Jesus better? Why?

2. What did Jesus do for the "less important" people: the woman who was a sinner; the man with the demons; the woman with a flow of blood?

3. How do these chapters answer further John's question to Jesus, "Are you the Messiah?"

CHOICES

Each person mentioned in these chapters has some choice to make about Jesus. For each there is some cost or sacrifice in coming to him. Those who recognize their need and Jesus' power are willing to break through barriers to come to him in faith and to follow him in obedience. What barriers stand between you and believing and following Jesus?

Discussion 5 / Luke 9, 10

Contrasts: Glory and Defeat, Rejection and Joy

Jesus now delegates power and authority to the twelve and sends them out to proclaim the kingdom of God and to heal. The issue of Jesus' identity and future comes to the fore, and he stresses the cost of being his disciple.

Luke 9:1-17

1. What do the three incidents in this section reveal about the increase of Jesus' popularity and the spread of his message?
2. What types of service are expected from the twelve (verses 1-6, 10-17)? What do Jesus' instructions (verses 3-6) suggest about the attitudes they are to have?

Luke 9:18-27

3. In this section Jesus confronts his disciples with a most important issue. What is required to answer Jesus' first question (verse 18)? What is required to answer his second question (verse 20)? Why are some people today able to answer only the first question?
4. What prophecy does Jesus give to his disciples in verse 22? What reason do you see for his waiting until this particular point to tell them what is going to happen to him?
5. What basic choice does Jesus say each man has? What are the results of this choice?

Luke 9:28-45

6. Describe the events that take place only eight days after Jesus has announced his coming suffering and death. What is

the purpose of going to the mountain? What is the subject of the conversation that Moses and Elijah have with Jesus? What is wrong with Peter's suggestion?

7. What problem have the other disciples been having down in the valley? Why?

8. In the light of the performance of the disciples in verses 28-43, what important fact does Jesus want to get through to them?

Luke 9:46-62

9. In contrast to the glory of the transfiguration, list the problems and disappointments which Jesus faces in this section. How would you describe the attitudes of Jesus' disciples here? What excuses do some potential disciples give to Jesus?

Luke 10:1-16

10. How does Jesus prepare the seventy for their ministry? What good and what bad results may they expect? What does *as lambs in the midst of wolves* indicate?

11. What strong warnings does Jesus give (verses 10-16)? Why? What is the purpose of his mighty works? What responsibility does the individual have who hears the message?

12. Explain the meaning of verse 16 and how it may apply today.

Luke 10:17-24

13. What gives the seventy joy? What additional promise does Jesus give them? What does he say they ought to rejoice in?

14. What joy does Jesus experience? Why? Why is Jesus the only way to come to know God?

15. According to verses 23, 24, why should all the disciples of Jesus be joyful? What ways do people today seek to find happiness? Happiness is seeing Jesus!

Luke 10:25-42

16. This section describes two people: a lawyer, and Jesus' friend Martha. Why does each approach Jesus? What does

each seek to prove? How does Jesus answer the lawyer? Martha? Describe persons today who have this lawyer's problem and those who have Martha's.

17. What is the good choice which Mary makes? What one thing is necessary in our lives?

SUMMARY

1. What did Jesus want his disciples to know, once they acknowledged him as the Messiah? What is the cost of discipleship? What are the joys?

2. If you were a reporter describing Jesus' ministry at this point in Luke's narrative, what difficulties would you indicate that Jesus faces?

CHOICES

The most important choice in a person's life is what he decides about Jesus the Christ of God. If you decide Jesus is who he claims to be and you commit your life to his lordship, then the rest of your life you will be making choices in the light of this one major decision. Mary made a good choice in a smaller situation because she had already made the most important choice of following Jesus.

Discussion 6 / Luke 11, 12

Harsh Words and Great Promises

Jesus' clear teachings bring strong reactions from the religious leaders of his day. He pronounces woes against them and warns his followers to avoid their mistakes.

Luke 11:1-13

1. Read the prayer Jesus teaches his disciples as if you had never heard it before. What impresses you about it? What does Jesus teach about the value of persistent prayer in the illustration he gives?
2. What encouragements to prayer does Jesus give? What does this section teach us about our heavenly Father?

Luke 11:14-28

3. What terrible accusation is made against Jesus? How does he answer it? What claim does Jesus make and what challenge?
4. In verses 24-26 what spiritual principle and warning does Jesus give?
5. How does Jesus correct the woman's praise in verses 27, 28? What does Jesus teach as necessary for those who follow him?

Luke 11:29-36

6. What indictment does Jesus make against the people of his generation? How may people like these crowds seeking sensational signs hinder the work of Jesus today? Why?
7. What point does Jesus make by comparing himself to Jonah and to Solomon? How had people responded to them? Why is Jesus' generation to be condemned?

8. What is the point of the warning Jesus gives in verses 33-36?

Luke 11:37-53

9. In verse 35 Jesus warned against thinking one is following the light when he is actually full of darkness. How does he go on to show that the Pharisees have done this? What do they emphasize? What do they neglect in their religious life?

10. What terrible accusations does Jesus make against the lawyers? What is the reaction of the religious leaders to Jesus' condemnation of their practices? Why?

Luke 12:1-12

11. According to 11:53, 54 and 12:1, what is the atmosphere in which Jesus declares the warnings to his disciples in verses 1-12? What are his warnings to them?

12. Whom should they not fear? Whom should they fear? Why? What is the point of the illustration in verses 6, 7? What temptation will Jesus' disciples face (verses 8-10)? Why shouldn't they be anxious at this prospect?

Luke 12:13-34

13. Describe the incident that causes Jesus to tell the parable in verses 16-21. What is the point of this parable? What was the rich man's chief concern? What should he have been concerned about? Analyze the concerns of most people today.

14. Why does Jesus tell us not to be anxious? What are we to do instead? What does *seek God's kingdom* mean to you? How does one accumulate heavenly treasure?

Luke 12:35-53

15. What does Jesus teach in verses 35-40? Why are faithfulness to Christ and readiness for his coming so important?

16. What is Jesus' answer to Peter's question (verse 41)? Why are those who know the will of God through his Word held more responsible?

17. Why and how does Jesus bring division on earth (verses 49-53)?

Luke 12:54-59

18. What does Jesus say the crowds are good at discerning? What do they fail to interpret? How would they live differently if they had spiritual discernment? Give an illustration of how Jesus' comments apply to people today.

19. What is the point about the court case (verses 57-59)? Why does Jesus want men to realize the need for settling their individual spiritual accounts with him by responding to him now? What warning is implied?

SUMMARY

1. Sum up the major warnings in this chapter. Why is it dangerous to ignore the claims of Jesus and their implications for us individually?

2. What are the words of comfort and guidance which stand out to you from this study?

CHOICES

Throughout today's study the descriptions of two ways of life are interwoven. One way is following Jesus. The other is not. The spiritual route we follow is determined by the choices we make.

Discussion 7 / Luke 13, 14

People in Danger; a Dinner Party

En route to Jerusalem Jesus encounters a variety of situations in which he teaches, heals, and warns people of the dangers of failure to respond to the kingdom of God when entrance is offered to them.

Luke 13:1-9

1. Of what does Jesus' warning in 12:57-59 remind some people? What question from them is implied? How does Jesus answer?
2. Using Old Testament imagery of the fig tree as a picture of the Jewish nation, what warning does Jesus give the nation in this parable? What should they do? What will happen if they don't?

Luke 13:10-17

3. Describe this incident on the sabbath in the synagogue. How does Jesus show that the attitude of the synagogue ruler is hypocritical and selfish? What tendency may we have toward this type of hypocrisy in the church today?

Luke 13:18-30

4. What do the two illustrations in verses 18-21 teach about the kingdom of God?
5. How does Jesus answer the question about the number of the saved? How does he change it from an academic discussion to a challenge? How can a person be sure not to be among those who are shut out?

Luke 13:31-35

6. How does Jesus respond to the Pharisees' warning that

Herod intends to kill him? Why isn't he deterred from his work? What hints does he give about the fact and the place of his death?

7. For whom is Jesus concerned? Why? What do you learn about Jesus from verses 33-35? What must we acknowledge about him? What will happen when we do this?

Luke 14:1-24

8. Describe the incident that occurs at the beginning of this dinner party. Why are the lawyers unable to accuse Jesus? How may we today care more for our "cattle" than for needy people? What is an appropriate use of the sabbath?

9. What does Jesus observe (verse 7) about the people at the party? What is the point of the parable he tells them? How can we avoid the tendency to exalt ourselves?

10. What parable does Jesus address to the host of the party? What reason does he give for inviting the needy instead of the rich? What does this help us to understand about the meaning of true hospitality?

11. Although one of the guests at the party shows enthusiasm for Jesus' teaching and for the kingdom of God, what does Jesus say in his next parable (verses 15-24)? See also Luke 9:57-62.

12. How do you think Jesus would tell this parable today? What excuses have you heard or seen for people not responding to Jesus' invitation?

13. What are our priorities and how are they expressed? What are Jesus' priorities?

Luke 14:25-33

14. What does it cost to follow Jesus? What three requirements does he mention? How do the two illustrations from building construction and from warfare explain why Jesus wants his followers to be realistic about the degree of commitment he requires?

Luke 14:34, 35

15. How does Jesus explain further why discipleship must

be of the quality described in verses 25-33? Why is something that looks like salt but is not salt of no worth?

16. Have you ever been disappointed by someone who lacked "saltness"?

SUMMARY

1. From chapter 13 find each instance of danger to individuals or groups. In your own words what dangers does Jesus warn about? What does he want people to do? Why?

2. If you were preaching a sermon on 13:35 what would you say about: a) your need; b) commitment to Jesus; c) assurance?

3. Tell a friend about the party you attend in 14:1-24.

CHOICES

Throughout these chapters Jesus is saying over and over again, directly and by parable, that he is inviting and urging people to come to him. He warns against rejecting his invitation or putting off responding to it.

Discussion 8 / Luke 15, 16

Lost Sinners, Poor and Rich

In this section Jesus uses parables to reveal God's attitude toward people considered outcasts by respectable religious people. He discusses faithfulness in the stewardship of what God has entrusted to us in possessions and relationships.

Luke 15:1-10

1. What types of people respond to the actions, teachings, and strong invitations Jesus has given in chapters 13, 14? Why do the Pharisees and the scribes object? Put their objections into contemporary terms.

2. How does Jesus' parable (verses 3-7) answer the objection the Pharisees and scribes have raised? What motivates the shepherd? What does Jesus say is his reason for spending time with tax collectors and sinners?

3. How do verses 8-10 follow the pattern of the previous parable? In each case what is lost? What is involved in seeking the lost? What happens when the lost is found? What is the spiritual truth which these parables teach? What is Jesus implying about the tax collectors and sinners?

Luke 15:11-32

4. Trace the steps in the younger brother's experience. What choices does he make along the way? What do you think motivates his various choices?

5. Compare the two sons who represent the two groups mentioned in verse 1. What are their sins? How do both of them experience alienation from their father? When does the younger son come to recognize his condition? What decision does he make? What happens upon his return?

6. Describe the father. How does he express his love for both his sons? What does he want for them both?

Luke 16:1-9

7. The parables in chapter 15 were a defense of the tax collectors and sinners who came to Jesus and of why Jesus accepted them. The parable in 16:1-9 may be told against the Pharisees. If so, how are the Pharisees being unfaithful stewards? How have they wasted the Lord's goods?

8. When does the steward change his attitude toward those below him? Why? What is he now ready to forgive? What basic warning is given in this parable?

Luke 16:10-15

9. Put into your own words the basic principles taught in this paragraph. Describe some of the opportunities we have today which test our faithfulness. Why are "little things" important?

10. Are you trying to do what Jesus says is impossible — to serve God and to serve the riches of this world?

11. Why do the religious leaders reject this teaching? If the same incident were repeated today, who would ridicule Jesus' words on this subject? Why?

12. In what way are the Pharisees acting out the very thing Jesus is saying? Whom are they trying to impress while they are supposed to be serving God?

Luke 16:16-31

13. Why do you think Jesus chooses to illustrate the importance of the law by referring to the commandment against adultery? Is there any other law he would choose today to emphasize the need for keeping the law of God? If not, why not?

14. What would you say are four major points of this parable (verses 19-31)? With whom in the parable would the Pharisees have to identify?

15. Compare verses 16, 17 and verse 31. Why is the law still valid even though many are responding to the good news

of the kingdom of God? What is the function of the law (verses 27-29)? See also Romans 3:19.

SUMMARY

1. What does chapter 15 reveal about God's attitude toward sinful men and what he wants for them?

2. What difference will (does) it make in your life that you recognize the Lord as your Shepherd and as your waiting, loving Father?

3. The theme of repentance is carried through both these chapters. See 15:7, 10, 18, 19; 16:30. What does it mean to *repent?* Why do all men need to repent? How do you know if you have experienced repentance (Luke 15:18, 20)?

CHOICES

Although we are left to speculate as to what choice the elder brother makes in response to his father, Jesus clearly indicates the wisdom of the younger brother's decision to change his mind and his way and to return to plead his father's mercy. Those who follow his example our heavenly Father graciously receives, forgives, and gives eternal life. (See Romans 6:23.)

Discussion 9 / Luke 17, 18

Preparing for Things to Come

In these two chapters Jesus prepares his disciples for the events which lie immediately ahead as they near Jerusalem and for all the days and years until his second coming.

Luke 17:1-10

1. What dire warning does Jesus give against being the one who causes others to sin? What is the difference between being tempted and tempting others to sin?
2. What responsibility do we have toward our fellow-Christians? Which do you find it harder to do — to rebuke or to forgive? Why?
3. Instead of the *quantity* of a man's faith, with what about that faith is Jesus more concerned (verses 5, 6)?
4. What does Jesus teach his disciples (verses 7-10) about the extent to which the servant of God must be willing to serve?

Luke 17:11-19

5. Where does this incident take place? What is Jesus' destination? What does the cry for mercy indicate about the one who asks for it? Describe the steps of the Samaritan leper's response to Jesus. What happened to the other nine lepers? Do you resemble the one or the nine in your attitudes toward God?
6. Title each of the four sections (verses 1-4, 5-6, 7-10, 11-19) with the specific Christian virtue which you think the section focuses upon. Give an illustration of the expression of these virtues today.

Luke 17:20-37

7. What is Jesus' two-fold answer to the Pharisees' question

as to when the kingdom of God would come?

8. In verses 22-37 for what three major times does Jesus prepare his disciples (verses 25, 22, 30)?

9. What does Jesus warn them about the period of time between his departure and his return (verses 22-23, 26-28)? Why should they mistrust any who claim that Jesus has returned here or there? What is the point of the simile in verse 24?

10. What characteristics did the people of Noah's day and those of Lot's day share? Why didn't they escape as Noah and Lot did? What point does Jesus make by these illustrations about being ready for his return? How does he strengthen his warning by verses 31-37?

How does verse 33 describe Lot's wife? What *life* did she want to hold on to? (Note — For background on Lot's wife see Genesis 19:17, 24-26.)

Luke 18:1-8

11. In light of what Jesus has been telling them in chapter 17, what do the disciples need? What things might cause them to lose heart?

12. What points about prayer does Jesus teach by his parable about the widow and the unrighteous judge? Why shouldn't Christians falter in their faith? What challenge is there to our generation in Jesus' question in verse 8?

Luke 18:9-14

13. How does Jesus continue his teaching about prayer? Why is it wrong to trust in oneself? Put the two prayers into your own words in a modern setting. What is wrong with the Pharisee's view of himself, of others, and of God?

Luke 18:15-30

14. Contrast the way the children come to Jesus and the way the ruler approaches him. How do children *receive?* What does the phrase *what shall I do* reveal about the ruler's understanding of eternal life? How is Jesus trying to elevate the ruler's idea of good by his challenge in verse 19?

15. About which of the commandments does Jesus *not* question the ruler? How does the command in verse 22 challenge the ruler on the first three of the ten commandments? See especially Exodus 20:3. What is this ruler's first love, his god?

16. What two major points does Jesus make about material riches in verses 24-30? Why is God never in our debt?

Luke 18:31-34

17. Review 9:21, 22, 30, 31; 13:33-35; 17:11, 25 to see how Luke is moving his narrative toward the coming events at Jerusalem. What new information does Jesus add in this paragraph to what he said in 9:22? What facts are repeated in both sections?

18. Why don't the twelve react to this information? Reflect on the aloneness Jesus must be experiencing.

Luke 18:35-43

19. When the blind man is told Jesus of Nazareth is going by, why doesn't he call Jesus by that name? What do the blind man's words in verse 38, repeated in verse 39, reveal about his view of himself and his understanding of who Jesus is? Why is *have mercy* always an appropriate prayer?

20. From verse 43 make a brief outline for a talk based on the verbs which describe the blind man's actions and the effect of his life on others.

SUMMARY

1. Summarize what you learn about the Christian life from these two chapters. What attitudes and actions does Jesus commend? What attitudes and actions does he condemn?

2. If you had only these two chapters, what would you know about Jesus? What power does he have? What promises does he make?

CHOICES

Consider the choices made by the Samaritan leper, the

ruler, and the blind man. There should be no such thing as a casual commitment to Jesus. He is worthy of and demands our whole selves, our time, our energies, our life. This total commitment is the only appropriate expression of our faith. Will he find it in you?

Discussion 10 / Luke 19; 20:1-18

Jericho, Jerusalem, and the Temple

In this section Jesus makes deliberate personal claims by his actions and his parables. When he reaches Jerusalem and begins teaching in the temple, members of the religious power-structure begin to take steps to get rid of him.

Luke 19:1-10

1. How do you account for the enthusiastic crowd which greets Jesus upon his entry into Jericho? (Remember the incident of 18:35-43.) If you were running for political office in Jericho against Zacchaeus what would you tell people about him? If you were Zacchaeus' campaign manager what would you say about him?

2. Compare the complaint (verse 7) and Jesus' answer (verse 10) with Luke 5:30-32; 7:39, 47; 15:2, 7, 10. What does each of Jesus' answers add to your understanding of who he is? In each case what do those who make the complaint fail to understand about Jesus?

3. How does Zacchaeus respond to the complaint in verse 7? In what other ways might he have responded? What does he openly acknowledge about himself?

Luke 19:11-27

4. What are the two reasons Jesus has for telling this parable? What don't the people or Jesus' disciples realize at this point?

5. Find at least six things about the nobleman in this parable. How does each also apply to Jesus? See also Luke 1:32, 33.

6. In the parable what is the difference between the servants and the citizens? What command does the nobleman

give his servants as to what they are to do during his absence? How does one of the servants fail to obey? Why? What is the result?

7. What is the reward given those who have worked for their master while he was away? What do you think is the reward for faithful Christian service?

8. How do the citizens of this parable become enemies? What happens to them? What does it mean to you to have Jesus reign in your life?

Luke 19:28-40

9. Having warned his disciples by the previous parable against false expectations of what would happen in Jerusalem, what preparations does Jesus make for his entry into the city?

10. What three titles are given to Jesus in this section. By whom and why is each given? Who initiates the entry into Jerusalem? Why do his followers greet him as they do (verses 37, 38)? Why doesn't Jesus rebuke his followers? What do the Pharisees imply by their demand?

Luke 19:41-48

11. Why does Jesus weep for Jerusalem? What does he foretell? What do the people of Jerusalem fail to recognize? Compare 19:44 with 17:20, 21.

12. Who does Jesus throw out of the temple and why? What is the reaction to his teaching in the temple? Why don't his enemies make their move at this point?

Luke 20:1-8

13. What challenge is put to Jesus as he teaches in the temple? By whom? What specific actions may they have in mind by *these things?*

14. Why does Jesus' question about their estimate of John's ministry put them into a dilemma?

Luke 20:9-18

15. What does Jesus claim about himself in this parable? How is this parable an answer to the Pharisees' question in

verse 2? What does Jesus predict their treatment of him will be?

16. What do the people realize Jesus is saying about Israel and its rulers by this parable? When they object to the point of the parable, what further truth does Jesus show them about himself from the Old Testament? What new picture do verses 17, 18 give of who Jesus is?

17. What does verse 18 teach about the judgment that will come to those who reject Jesus? What two choices do people have about what to do with the stone which is Jesus?

SUMMARY

1. In this study we have considered two major parables (19:11-27 and 20:9-18) which Jesus spoke and one "parable" which he acted out (19:28-40). What themes do you find recurring? What conclusions can you draw from these observations?

2. What difference do Jesus' claims make to you personally?

CHOICES

Zacchaeus is like the person today who is rich, successful, part of the establishment, yet who has a hunger to find spiritual reality. Many are like Zacchaeus, almost hanging out of trees in their eagerness to see Jesus. It is when they, like Zacchaeus, respond to the command of Jesus and choose to obey him that their lives are transformed.

Discussion 11 / Luke 20:19-47; 21

Temple Teachings and Predictions

The exchanges in the temple continue in this section as Jesus answers questions intended to destroy him. Beginning at 20:41, he turns and delivers warnings and prophecies about the fall of Jerusalem and about his second coming.

Luke 20:19-26

1. What do the scribes and the chief priests understand about the parables in verses 9-18? What keeps them from acting against Jesus? What are their spies supposed to accomplish for them? (Compare with 18:31-33.)

2. Into what political trap is their first question (verse 22) intended to snare Jesus? Why would they think that their question will catch Jesus no matter which way he answers?

3. How does Jesus confound them by his answer? What things are Caesar's in your life? What things belong to God?

Luke 20:27-40

4. Who now challenges Jesus? How is their hypocrisy and their mockery revealed by the question they choose to pose? (What is their belief about the resurrection?)

5. Although the question apparently is asked in ridicule, how does Jesus answer it (verses 34-36)? What does Jesus go on to teach concerning the resurrection? How does Jesus prove the reality of resurrection by his reference to the law of Moses which the Saduccees accept as Scripture?

6. Since his arrival in Jerusalem and his teaching in the temple, what three major questions have been asked Jesus? (See Luke 20:2, 22, 33.) Would you say the quality of the

questions is improving or diminishing? Why?

Luke 20:41 to 21:4

7. Jesus now turns to challenge his hearers with a question. Why have they been holding too low a view of Messiah? How does Jesus prove that Messiah is greater, not less than David?

8. What is Jesus' description of the scribes? How would this description be given today? What effect would religious leaders like this have upon the people? Why is it dangerous to be responsible for "turning people off" spiritually?

9. How does Jesus compare the gifts of the rich with the gift of the poor widow?

Luke 21:5-9

10. What startling statement does Jesus make? What part does the temple play in the Jews' religious and national life of that day? What would its destruction mean? What do the hearers want to know and how does Jesus answer? What danger must Jesus' followers avoid?

Note — Jesus' words concerning the temple were fulfilled in A.D. 70 at the fall of Jerusalem when 1,100,000 Jews died, 97,000 were taken away into captivity, and Jewish national life came to an end for almost 1900 years.

Luke 21:10-19

11. What types of calamities does Jesus foretell in verses 10, 11? Who would be affected?

12. When are the events of verses 12-19 to take place? What does Jesus indicate is to happen to his followers? Why will they be persecuted and by whom? What opportunity comes with persecution? What promises does Jesus give his persecuted followers?

13. How do you explain verses 18, 19 in the light of verse 16?

Luke 21:20-24

14. Describe the events foretold in this paragraph. What

specific instructions are given? Why would most Jews flee into the city rather than away from it?

15. What does Jesus say will happen to the Jews at the destruction of Jerusalem? How long will Jerusalem be in Gentile hands? What does the return of Jerusalem to the Jews signal?

Luke 21:25-28

16. After the times of the Gentiles what things will begin to happen (verses 25, 26)? What effect will these events have on people?

17. For what are the events of verses 25, 26 a prelude? What causes for rejoicing do verses 27, 28 suggest?

Luke 21:29-38

18. How does Jesus emphasize the need for watchfulness? What kind of life is inappropriate for his followers? Why? How do our hearts become weighed down? How should we prepare for *that day?*

19. What pattern does Jesus follow during the week after his triumphal entrance into Jerusalem (verses 37, 38)?

SUMMARY

1. From 20:19-47 describe the continuing confrontations Jesus has in the temple. What do you think is happening?

2. Summarize what you learn from chapter 21 about:
   - the predicted destruction of the temple and the fall of Jerusalem,
   - the persecution of the followers of Christ,
   - the end time and Jesus' return in glory.

How does Jesus instruct his followers in the light of these events?

3. What quality of life ought to characterize Christians living in the present days of pressure and distress?

CHOICES

In chapter 21 events are described over which the people

involved have no control. They cannot choose whether they wish to suffer persecution, whether the temple will be destroyed, etc. The choice involved is how the followers of Jesus will respond to these unavoidable circumstances.

This is often true in our daily lives as well. God may not change our difficult circumstances but he can and will change us in our circumstances as we choose to trust and obey him.

Discussion 12 / Luke 22, 23

Last Supper, Trials, Crucifixion

Luke has ended his account of Jesus' teachings in the temple and now describes step by step the events which bring Jesus to his death on the cross.

Luke 22:1-23

1. Ask someone to review briefly the events of the first Passover (Exodus 12:1-39). Of what should the celebration of the feast remind the Jews?

2. What contrasts do you observe between the people, plans, and purposes described in this section? What motivates Judas?

Note — The man with the water jar is probably a prearranged signal since normally only women of that day would carry water jars.

3. What arrangement is made between the Jewish leaders and Judas? What reason do you see for Jesus' secrecy about the place where he will have the Passover supper? What does verse 15 indicate of Jesus' attitude toward his disciples?

4. What five things does Jesus reveal to his disciples in verses 16-22? How and to what do they react in verse 23? How many potential betrayers do you think are there?

Luke 22:24-38

5. What lack of sensitivity (verse 24) do the disciples exhibit toward Jesus in what he is facing? What is their concern?

6. How does Jesus' teaching on greatness conflict with the world's idea of greatness? How has he illustrated the concept of true greatness which he teaches? Suggest ways in which we today can serve in the manner the Lord desires.

7. What do verses 28-30 suggest about the rewards of faithful service? Compare with Luke 19:17.

8. What glimpse do you get into the spiritual conflict over Simon Peter (verses 31, 32)? What is foretold about Peter and what commission is given to him? What conflict is there between Peter's idea of himself and Jesus' knowledge of him in verses 33, 34?

9. What drastic change is about to come into the disciples' lives (verses 35-38)?

Luke 22:39-53

10. What does Jesus tell his disciples before and after he prays? What does this suggest about what this experience means to Jesus himself? See Luke 4:13. What is Jesus' prayer?

11. Describe the events related in verses 47-53. What incongruities do you observe?

Luke 22:54-71

12. What indicates Peter's bravery and his cowardice? What discovery does Peter make about himself? Why are we always shocked when we fall? What comfort is it to realize that the Lord is not shocked?

13. Describe the atmosphere in verses 63-65.

14. In verses 66-71 what two questions does Jesus answer affirmatively? What claims does he make? What case against Jesus does the assembly of elders now believe they have?

Luke 23:1-25

15. What accusations does the Jewish council make against Jesus before Pilate? (Luke has previously mentioned Pilate in 3:1; 13:1.) What evidence is there that they know their accusation concerning tribute is a lie (see 20:19-26)?

16. Trace the decisions Pilate makes (verses 4, 14, 16, 22, 24), and the reasons for his decisions. Why do you think Pilate sends Jesus to Herod? What is Herod's attitude and why is he frustrated? Why do you think Herod and Pilate become friends that day?

Luke 23:26-56

17. Compare Simon of Cyrene, the women, the rulers, the soldiers, the two criminals, the centurion, and Joseph of Arimathea in what each has to do with Jesus.

18. What does Jesus say to: the women, his Father, the criminal on the cross, and again to his Father? Why doesn't Jesus respond to the challenges in verses 35, 37, 39? Why could they be considered Jesus' last temptation?

19. What unusual events does Luke record in verses 44, 45? What do you learn about Joseph (verses 50-53)? Why can the women do nothing immediately about Jesus' body?

SUMMARY

1. Compare Peter and Judas. What similarities and what differences do you observe between them? What do you think made the difference between these two disciples who were both witnesses to the acts and words of Jesus during his public ministry?

2. What do you observe about Jesus throughout these two chapters? What are his concerns, his emotions, his attitudes? What difference does this make to you?

CHOICES

In today's study three men made choices about Jesus which affect what happens to Jesus and the dimension of his suffering, and ensure that they themselves will be known throughout future history. Surely none of the three — Judas, Peter, or Pilate — had the slightest inkling of the vast significance of the choices they made.

This is often true for us. We make choices under the pressure of the moment but the results have far-reaching ramifications. Every choice made concerning Jesus Christ is of ultimate consequence for the person who makes the decision.

ASSIGN review questions to be prepared during the coming week. See page 63.

Discussion 13 / Luke 24; Review; Resurrection!

The last chapter of Luke's Gospel describes how Jesus' disciples discover the evidences and the reality of his resurrection. Luke prepares his readers for the second volume of his account (Acts) by describing the risen Lord's instructions to his followers to be his witnesses and messengers.

Luke 24:1-12

1. According to 23:49, 55, what have the women experienced? What emotions do you imagine they have as they go to the tomb? See Mark 16:3 to understand one of their concerns. What is their intention in coming to the tomb when the sabbath is over?
2. Upon their arrival at the tomb, what two discoveries do they make? How do they react to the appearance of the two men?
3. What report do the women make to the other disciples and how is it received? What does this indicate about the expectation of the eleven and the rest? What do you observe about Luke's restraint in dealing with Judas (verse 9)?
4. How does Peter check on the women's report (verse 12)? What is his reaction to what he discovers?

Luke 24:13-27

5. What are the two discussing on their way to Emmaus? What do you think would be included in their conversation? Why don't they recognize Jesus when he joins them? If you were filming this incident how would you show this scene? What do the two tell Jesus in answer to his question?
6. How do you know that they have lost hope in spite of the women's report? How would you have reacted in their place? Why?
7. What fault does Jesus find with these disciples? Note that their statement in 24:21 implies that they had believed Je-

sus to be the fulfillment of the Old Testament promise of a redeemer.

8. Why would Jesus want to interpret to them the Old Testament prophecies about himself before they recognize him? What is the scope of his teaching (verse 27) and its point (verse 26)? Why is it essential that they understand what the Scripture teaches about the Christ?

Luke 24:28-35

9. Why does Jesus go to the home of these disciples? What does their invitation indicate about them?

10. Whose position at table does Jesus assume (verse 30)? Why do you think that this is the moment they recognize him? (See also Luke 9:16.)

11. What do the two remember about their conversation with Jesus on the road to Emmaus? Why do they return to Jerusalem? What do they learn upon their return? What do they report? Imagine the emotions of those present that evening.

Luke 24:36-43

12. What does Jesus understand about his troubled disciples? How does he allay their fears and questions? What proofs does he offer?

13. What does this section indicate about the kind of resurrection Luke reports? Why is this clearly *not* a resurrection in which "he lives on in the hearts of his followers"?

Luke 24:44-53

14. What do you learn about Jesus' teaching ministry (verse 44)? What do you learn about the Scriptures? Compare verses 27 and 45. In each case what does Jesus do for his disciples?

15. List ten things Jesus teaches in verses 46-51. What things are already accomplished? What things are to be done? What and why are Jesus' disciples responsible to preach? How will they be able to meet this task?

16. Describe Jesus' departure and the disciples' reaction to it.

SUMMARY

1. What hard evidence do the disciples receive in this chapter to prove the reality of Jesus' resurrection? What clear indications do you find that they were not preconditioned to expect the resurrection of Jesus?

2. From the things he says and does, what are the priorities of the risen Lord Jesus? How do these priorities apply to you?

CHOICES

The Roman world knew something about extravaganzas and how to sweep the populace along in a grand display of power. Rome used the show of arms, the power of music, mob psychology. They could influence the populace in the same ways governments today influence their people through the mass media.

Man tries to make his little insignificant things seem large and important by sensational exploitation . Consider what our God is like who chooses to "produce" the most spectacular event in human history in the way described in this chapter.

Review of Luke 1 through 24

Assign each person in the group one of these questions to prepare and share his findings. Ask everyone to prepare question 7.

1. What do you learn from Luke's detailed description of the events surrounding the birth of Jesus? Summarize.
2. Describe the temptations of Jesus and his response to temptation. What do you learn from Jesus' experience about how to overcome temptation?
3. Trace the training and experience of Jesus' disciples. Summarize what you think Jesus wanted them to know and to be.
4. Select three people described by Luke whose lives were completely transformed because they met Jesus. Share the insights you find from studying their experience.
5. List the major points Jesus makes by his longer parables in Luke's Gospel.
6. Beginning at Luke 19:28, outline briefly the major teachings of Jesus during the week before his death on the cross.
7. What connection do you see between the events in this book and your own life? For some direction in your thinking, see Luke 24:46, 47; 1 Peter 1:18-21; Romans 3:21-26; Isaiah 53:5-12; 1 Corinthians 15:3-5.

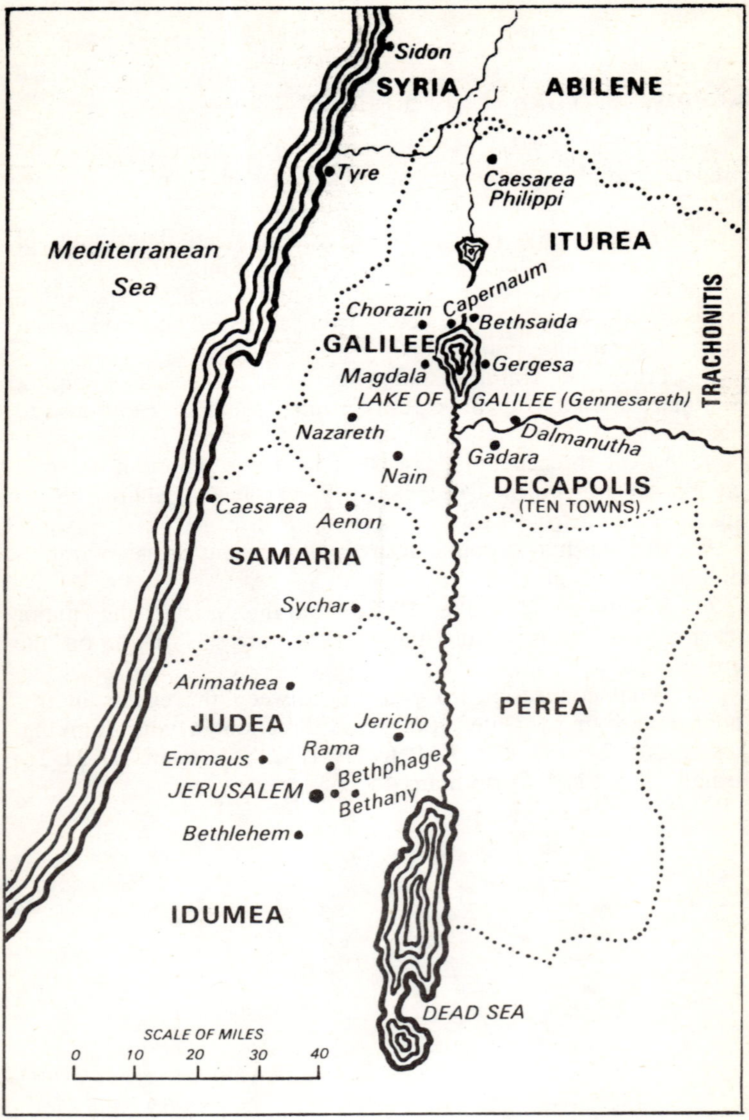
Sidon
SYRIA
ABILENE
Tyre
Caesarea
Philippi
ITUREA
Mediterranean
Sea
TRACHONITIS
Chorazin
Capernaum
Bethsaida
GALILEE
Gergesa
Magdala
LAKE OF GALILEE (Gennesareth)
Nazareth
Dalmanutha
Gadara
Nain
DECAPOLIS
(TEN TOWNS)
Caesarea
Aenon
SAMARIA
Sychar
Arimathea
PEREA
JUDEA
Jericho
Rama
Emmaus
Bethphage
JERUSALEM
Bethany
Bethlehem
IDUMEA
DEAD SEA
SCALE OF MILES
0
10
20
30
40